George Washington Carver

Jennifer Strand

abdopublishing.com

Published by Abdo Zoom™, PO Box 398166, Minneapolis, Minnesota 55439. Copyright © 2017 by Abdo Consulting Group, Inc. International copyrights reserved in all countries. No part of this book may be reproduced in any form without written permission from the publisher. Abdo Zoom™ is a trademark and logo of Abdo Consulting Group, Inc.

Printed in the United States of America, North Mankato, Minnesota
072016
092016

THIS BOOK CONTAINS RECYCLED MATERIALS

Cover Photo: AP Images
Interior Photos: AP Images, 1, 5, 12–13, 18; Midwest National Parks, 6; Robert Amendola/George Washington Carver National Monument, 7; National Park Service, 8–9; People Images/iStockphoto, 9; Frances Benjamin Johnston/ Library of Congress, 10, 11, 14; iStockphoto, 12, 17; US National Archives and Records Administration, 15; Bettmann/ Getty Images, 16; Arthur Rothstein/FSA/OWI Collection/Library of Congress, 19

Editor: Emily Temple
Series Designer: Madeline Berger
Art Direction: Dorothy Toth

Publisher's Cataloging-in-Publication Data
Names: Strand, Jennifer, author.
Title: George Washington Carver / by Jennifer Strand.
Description: Minneapolis, MN : Abdo Zoom, [2017] | Series: Incredible inventors
    | Includes bibliographical references and index.
Identifiers: LCCN 2016941403 | ISBN 9781680792294 (lib. bdg.) |
    ISBN 9781680793970 (ebook) | 9781680794861 (Read-to-me ebook)
Subjects: LCSH: Carver, George Washington, d1864?-1943--Juvenile
    literature. | African American agriculturists--Biography--Juvenile literature--
    | Agriculturists--Biography--Juvenile literature.
Classification: DDC 630.92 [B]--dc23
LC record available at http://lccn.loc.gov/2016941403

Table of Contents

Introduction

George Washington Carver was an African-American scientist. He helped people grow plants. He found new ways to use them.

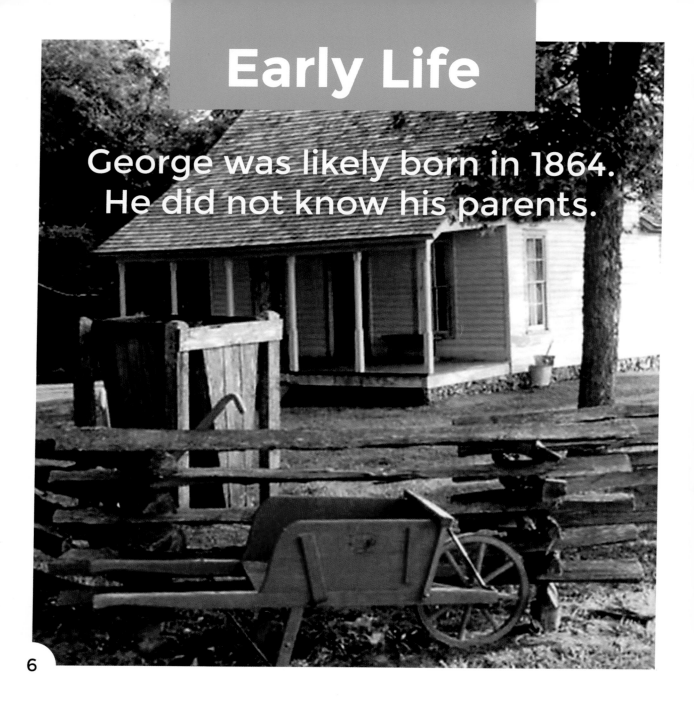

Early Life

George was likely born in 1864. He did not know his parents.

He was born into slavery.
Moses and Susan Carver
owned him.

Slavery ended. George moved to the family's house.

Susan Carver taught George.
He was curious. He studied plants.

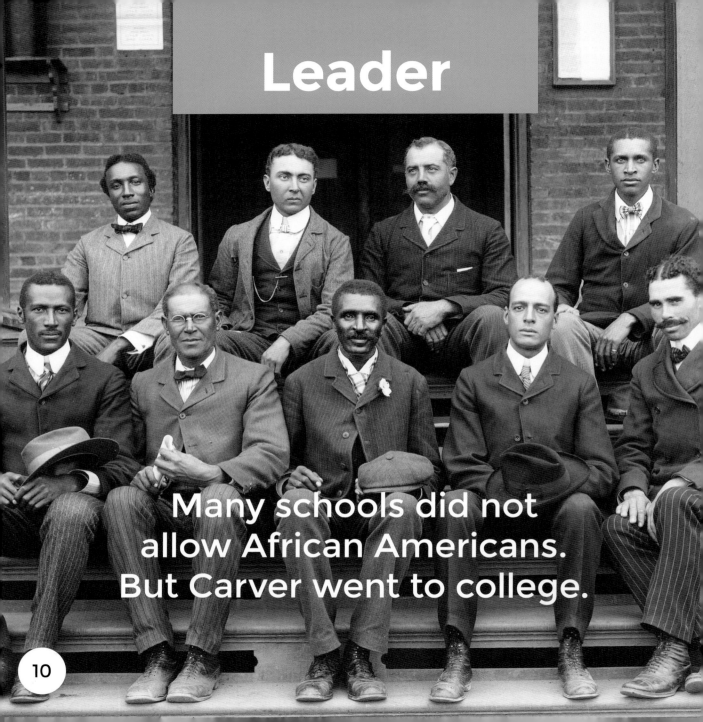

Leader

Many schools did not allow African Americans. But Carver went to college.

He studied agriculture.
He found new ways to farm.

Carver studied peanut plants.

He used them to make
soil healthy. He found
many ways to use peanuts.

Carver wanted to share
what he learned.

So he started the
Agriculture Movable School.
It taught people how to farm well.

Carver started crop rotation.
Farmers could plant different crops.
This kept the soil healthy.

Legacy

Carver died on January 5, 1943. His work helped people reduce waste.

This protected **natural resources**.
It also helped many people.

Quick Stats

George Washington Carver

Born: around 1864

Birthplace: Diamond Grove, Missouri

Known For: Carver was an African-American scientist and conservationist.

Died: January 5, 1943

1864: George Washington Carver is born around this time.

1890: Carver attends Simpson College in Iowa.

1896: Carver becomes director of agriculture at Tuskegee Institute.

1921: Carver speaks to the US Congress about peanuts.

1939: President Franklin D. Roosevelt gives Carver a medal for his discoveries in science.

1943: Carver dies on January 5.

Glossary

agriculture - the raising of crops or animals.

crop rotation - growing different crops in the same space in an order that keeps the soil healthy.

natural resources - materials produced by the earth that are necessary or useful to people.

slavery - the practice of buying and owning other people against their will.

Booklinks

For more information on **George Washington Carver**, please visit booklinks.abdopublishing.com

 In on Biographies!

Learn even more with the Abdo Zoom Biographies database. Check out abdozoom.com for more information.

Index